Table of Contents

The Foundation

"You are always with your younger self" - Jon Saxx

Chapter 1 - Who, What and Why

Who is This Book For?

- The student who_____

_____

Who is the Author?
EXERCISE: What have I learned about the author? *(Page 4)*

_____

_____

_____

Question Everything?

- After being given the Webster definition of 'ignorance'', how can I apply to myself what the author teaches about SHEEP? *(Page 4)*

_____

_____

_____

EXERCISE: Mom and the Ham Story *(Page 5)*
- Write an example. Something I learned about a habit or tradition in my family.

_____

_____

_____

Change the Way You Ask Questions *(Page 7)*

- Curiosity is more than asking "Why?" Learn how to ask better questions to gain better responses
- Use a calm demeanor to minimize potentially upsetting who I am speaking with

EXERCISE: Create your own example of changing "Why" to "What"

- *"Why did you do that?"*

   Translates to _____

- *"Why are you...?"*

  Translates to _____

- *"Why can't you just...?"*

  Translates to _____

Four Levels of Competence *(Page 8)*

- **TIP:** Learning happens in different phases. Trust the process!

EXERCISE: Write a definition for each *'Phase of Competence'* on the lines below. Give your own example of each.

> **Unconsciously Incompetent**

_____

_____

_____

> **Consciously Incompetent**

_____

_____

_____

> **Consciously Competent**

_____

_____

_____

> **Unconsciously Competent**

_____

_____

_____

EXERCISE: Self-Reflection Questions *(Page 9)*

Take time to reflect and write your honest answers.

1. Who am I? *(think about my identity, labels, and titles I hold)*

_____

_____

2. What problem in the world am I passionate about solving?

_____

_____

3. What does success look like to me?

_____

_____

4. What have I failed in? & What lessons did I learn from the failure?

_____

_____

5. Who are my mentors? *(Are they leading me to where I want to go?)*

_____

_____

6. What are my addictions and habits? *(Are they positive or negative, healthy or unhealthy?)*

_____

_____

7. Who am I following and listening to, including social media, music, and real life?

_____

_____

8. What advice would I give my younger self? *(In two words? In one sentence?)*

_____

_____

_____

Chapter 2 - Adolescence

Influences *(Page 11)*

EXERCISE: Think about and write the qualities, habits, and phrases my parents, relatives, and friends possess that influence me the most

List Qualities –
  Positive: **Negative:**

_____   _____

_____   _____

List Habits –
  Good: **Bad:**

_____   _____

_____   _____

List Phrases –
  Positive: **Negative:**

_____   _____

_____   _____

- From the above what do I sometimes see myself doing, demonstrating, or saying?

_____   _____

_____   _____

Childhood *(Page 12)*

Dear _____ *(write name here)*

"Stop limiting yourself based on what people think about you!
Love yourself and embrace who you were created to be."

QUESTION: What can I personally apply from the author's letter about limiting myself ?

_____

_____

_____

_____

Positive Role Models *(Page 13)*

EXERCISE:

- Name of a male figure who has taught or can teach me important life skills, lessons, and words of wisdom.

_____

- Name of a female figure who has taught or can teach me important life skills, lessons, and words of wisdom.

_____

- Here are two things *(life skills, lessons, or words of wisdom)* I have learned from both:

_____

_____

_____

The Benefits of Teacher Relationships *(Page 16)*

EXERCISE: What did the author learn about teacher relationships? How can I apply this advice to my life and schooling?

_____

_____

_____

_____

Eighth Grade *(Page 18)*

ENTREPRENEURSHIP EXERCISE:

List some ways I can earn money as a teenager:

_____

_____

_____

What are some ways I currently earn money?

_____   _____

_____   _____

The Six Secrets of Persuasion *(Page 19)*

- **Hint:** Sometimes in life you have to work backwards...

- **SIX**
- **SECRETS**
- **PERSUASION**
- **LIKING**
- **SCARCITY**
- **CONSENSUS**
- **RECIPROCITY**
- **CONSISTENCY**
- **AUTHORITY**

A	Q	S	T	E	R	C	E	S	R	B	O
U	M	I	T	R	U	O	F	L	E	N	A
T	X	L	I	K	I	N	G	A	C	O	K
H	P	O	I	L	B	S	T	R	I	I	W
O	Y	Y	P	E	T	E	H	B	P	S	H
R	V	T	E	A	R	N	B	W	R	A	L
I	U	S	I	X	N	S	G	F	O	U	U
T	D	L	W	C	B	U	Z	X	C	S	V
Y	F	R	N	E	R	S	M	K	I	R	T
E	L	A	J	I	H	A	P	Y	T	E	S
S	Z	C	I	T	H	E	C	D	Y	P	H
Y	Y	C	N	E	T	S	I	S	N	O	C

The Power of Sound *(Pages 22 – 23)*

- *"IT IS COOL TO MARCH TO YOUR OWN BEAT!"*
- *"Be conscious of what you allow to enter your ears."*

QUESTION: What is one point I would share with someone from this section?

_____

_____

MUSICAL EXERCISE:

Write some of the lyrics from one or two of your favorite songs!

_____

_____

_____

_____

_____

What is the personal meaning of these lyrics and how do you apply them to your life?

_____

_____

_____

_____

_____

Create your own lyrics or write a poem! These lyrics do not have to rhyme. **Express yourself!**

_____

_____

_____

_____

_____

_____

_____

_____

_____

High School

"Everybody has a different puzzle, man. You just got to figure out your own puzzle." - Kobe Bryant

Chapter 3 - Post Secondary Preparation

EXERCISE: Self-Assessment Questions *(Page 28)*

- What do I genuinely want to do after high school? ***Be honest.*** What are the people I admire doing, wearing, and reading? What did they do to get where they are today?

_____

_____

_____

- What is currently available and within reach to help make sure what I want to do after high school becomes a reality? *(Ex: mentors, teachers, alumni, books, videos, etc.)*

_____

_____

- What are my academic goals? *(certain GPA, graduate in the top 10, etc.)*

_____

_____

- *Favorite Class/Subject* _____

- *Least Favorite Class/Subject* _____

- *Best Class/Subject* _____

- *Worst Class/Subject* _____

- *Why? (Best & Worst)* _____

    _____

- *What have I done to get help if I need it?* _____

- *Do I plan to go to college? If yes, where?* _____

    _____

- *Public or Private?* _____

- *In-State or Out of State?* _____

- *Approximate Cost per year?* _____

- *How will I pay for it? (FAFSA, Scholarships, etc.)* _____

  _____

- *GPA or Test Scores needed?* _____

- *What are my extracurricular goals? (sports, orgs, clubs, gain employment)*

  _____

  _____

  _____

- What are the **top three distractions** that take time and energy away from achieving my goals?

  1) _____

  2) _____

  3) _____

- Do my family and friends support and respect my dreams and the sacrifices I must make to achieve them?

  _____

  _____

ASSIGNMENT:

Interview one (1) family member **and** one (1) friend. Ask each person you interview the following questions. Write down their responses.

1) Do you support my dreams to become a _____?

2) Thinking of my desires, skills, and talents, what other careers do you believe I would be well suited for? _____

_____

3) What sacrifices do you believe I must make to achieve my career goals?

_____

_____

Paying Attention to Your Environment *(Page 29):* We typically become the average of the (5) five people we spend the most time with. Write their names.

_____   _____

_____   _____

_____

What does who I spend the most time with say about me?

_____

Who will I choose to follow and interact with to elevate myself?

_____

Leveraging School and Defining Success *(Page 30)*

Success is not an accident. What is my definition of SUCCESS?

_____

_____

The Illusion of Time *(Page 32)*

🔑 **Ninth Grade** – Create a solid foundation
  - Establish a good GPA
  - Avoid low grades
  - Have a motivating friend group
  - Build a positive reputation (academics & character)
  - Build positive relationships with teachers, coaches, counselors, etc.

🔑 **Tenth Grade**
  - Continue building or improve upon what you did in ninth grade
  - If your school allows, decide if you want to attend a trade or vocational school

🔑 **Eleventh Grade** – Who is paying attention to me?
  - Know your transcript
  - Take ACT and/or SAT
  - Attend College Tours
  - Think about your future major

🔑 **Twelfth Grade** – This is IT! Swimming in the "real world" soon!
  4 Questions to Ask Myself *(Page 35)*

- _____

- _____

- _____

- _____

16

The 4 Es of Postgrad Options *(Page 35)*

★ **E1: Enrollment** – Interview two current college students. Ask what they have learned about:

- Finances
- Needed ACT/SAT scores
- Course load
- Application process
- Their major
- Lessons learned

Reponses Received:

_____

_____

_____

QUESTION: What are my main reasons for wanting to attend college? *(if I choose to go)*

_____

_____

_____

★ **E2: Employment** – a person who is hired to work for a business, in return for payment

QUESTION: What are some opportunities of being paid to learn?

_____   _____

_____   _____

_____   _____

★ **E3: Entrepreneurship** – a person who owns, organizes, and operates a business while taking on greater than normal financial risks. *(Page 38)*

EXERCISE: *(Fill in the blanks)*

- If I choose this route, be sure to have a _____

- I must analyze my _____

- _____ can be sold.

ASSIGNMENT: Pretend you are going to start a business. Businesses can sell products, services, experiences, information, or commodities.

What am I going to sell? _____

How am I going to sell it? _____

Who is my target customer? _____

What are the start up costs? _____

What other businesses can I study to learn how they became successful? _____

_____

★ **E4: Enlistment** – The military is another option for students who are uncertain about what they want to do with their lives.

EXERCISE: Circle all the benefits serving in the military could result in. (Page 40)

- Free Travel
- Insurance
- Housing
- Create Your Own Schedule

- Clothing
- Healthcare
- Store Discounts
- Culinary Training

- Meet New People
- College Financial Assistance
- Special Interest Rates
- Guaranteed Employment

A Combination of Es

- *"I am allowed to choose more than one of the 4 Options of E's"*

EXERCISE: Of the 4 Es – Circle two (2) that are of greatest interest to you.

Enrollment   Employment   Entrepreneurship   Enlistment

The Journey of Deciding *(Page 40)*

Every choice has pros and cons. It would be very wise of me to take the necessary time to figure out what is best for me.

Try new things!   Take initiative!

Discover your passion!   Be open to various possibilities!

Use your resources!   Learn what is necessary!

"We are all entrepreneurs and **I AM THE CEO OF MY LIFE!** Even if I become an employee, my employer is my 'largest' client... but not my only."

How do I figure out what I want to do? *(Fill in the blanks)*

- Visualize and question _____

- Gain experience in jobs, _____.

- After I figure out what problems I am passionate about solving, then I should:

  - find a _____ that allows me to do so **-or-**

  - create a _____ to do it how I envision

Book Reference: *"Rich & Righteous"* by Jullien Gordon *(Page 42)*

ASSIGNMENT: Read the book excerpt on Page 42. Write down what you take away from the message in the excerpt:

_____

_____

_____

_____

My Job Experiences *(Page 42)*

ASSIGNMENT: List the job(s) or even volunteer experience(s) you have had. What did you learn from each job? [examples: cashier, cutting grass, community events]

_____

_____

_____

_____

_____

_____

_____

Chapter 4 - My Personal Experience

> ***A widely held but incorrect stigma:*** *"Students who choose to attend trade or vocational school, do not go to college."* This is false! Students who attend and graduate from a trade school can still attend a university and flourish!

The Love of Basketball *(Page 46)*

- ***Words of wisdom to athletes***... *"my training should be similar to how I will move my body in my preferred or main sport."*
- I should perform with confidence no matter who is looking or what others might think

College Student *(Page 54)*

- *"Growing up, I saw that those around me who were celebrated by others and seemed to be enjoying life to the fullest, either were in college or had graduated from college."*

QUESTIONS:

1. What eye-opening reality did the author learn about his family's finances?

_____

2. Ask your parent(s) what the plan or strategy is to pay for your college tuition and

expenses if you eventually decide to enroll. Write what they say:_____

_____

_____

3. Which college tuition is normally more expensive? *(Check √ one)*

In state *(of my residence)* _____

Out of state *(of my residence)* _____

4. Which colleges do I plan to apply to? _____

_____

_____

**College Athlete (*Page 57)*

*"Simple does not mean easy. If I truly want something, I must **GO GET IT!**"*

EXERCISE:
Give an example of a time when you wanted something, and you decided to **"GO GET IT!"**

- What I wanted was: _____

- Potential or actual roadblocks, or moments of difficulty were: _____

  _____

- How I went about obtaining it: _____

  _____

- I should believe in myself, no matter what my age is!
- My GPA is a large factor in how much money I can earn to pay for college, and even put directly into my bank account! However, it would be wise and beneficial to still challenge myself by taking some seemingly difficult or college credit courses while I am still in high school.

QUESTIONS:

- What is my current GPA? _____
- When I graduate from high school, I want my GPA to be a _____
- Do I want to become a college athlete? _____
- If yes, which sport? _____
- To accomplish my GPA goal and/or my college athletics goal, here are the things I will need to do before I graduate high school:

  _____

  _____

  _____

  _____

  _____

  _____

Chapter 5 - The System

Tap in and unleash the power of your mind. Adopting a rich vocabulary has a way of unleashing that power. More regions of the brain are strengthened in vocabulary tasks. Try this exercise and expand your mind!

EXERCISE:

- Take notes while you read today *(a textbook, homework problems, social media caption, a book for leisure, etc.)*
- Write down one unfamiliar word, find the definition, and then try using that word 5 times

The word I was not familiar with and chose to use is:

_____

One way I used that word is:

_____

- I can obtain my desired job or salary and much more by:
    - properly leveraging school
    - expanding my network
    - gaining meaningful experiences
    - fine-tuning my ability to properly market myself

Mathematics *(Page 66)*

- Rephrasing questions is a strategy to better understand and solve problems in any subject. A high level course like Calculus is more about critical thinking than numbers.
- We live in a universe that revolves around mathematics.
- When I have difficulty understanding something or accomplishing a large assignment, it is beneficial to find ways to break it down into a simpler form.
- *"If I have time to watch TV, be on social media or go to parties, then I have time to accomplish tasks that will positively benefit my future."*

Digital Pros and Cons *(Page 67)*

- A good strategy is deleting social media apps during times of extreme focus. This will help reduce the urges to scroll, which could actually help me in the process of achieving my goals. Replace the scrolling time with studying for academics, athletics, or business.
- Another strategy is using social media for learning beneficial and applicable information while also connecting with experts in different fields
- Keep in mind, distractions will still pop up. Learn to mitigate those distractions.

The **Four Es of Content** I should be conscious of *(Page 68)*

EXERCISE: Write down the definition of each word below; include what you think too

Educate: _____

_____

Entertain: _____

_____

Eroticize: _____

_____

Escape: _____

_____

ASSIGNMENT: Use these points as your checklist. Check off √ when you have done each point and the date you have accomplished it.

Point #1	**Establish a bio that quickly tells who I am and post content that resembles what I represent.**
• ___ *Date Accomplished*_____	
Point #2	**Turn off social media notifications.**
• ___ *Date Accomplished*_____	
Point #3	**Reach out to some experts in a topic I am interested in.**
• ___ *Date Accomplished*_____	

Meditation and Metacognition *(Page 70)*

- Anything that brings me peace and some type of quietness or stillness can be classified as

  _____.

- It is a healthy choice and daily practice to remove myself from others or any technological distractions for at least 5 minutes a day.

- During the time away from technology, I can relax, reflect, and focus on my breathing.

- _____ is the process of thinking about, what I am thinking about.
- Questioning myself and the thoughts that pop up into my mind is also metacognition
- It is wise to evaluate what I allow to occupy my mind. *(This level of intention allows us to respond to situations based on logic instead of reacting too quickly based on emotions)*
- Mindfulness activities can be an engaging way to increase self-awareness

AWARENESS EXERCISE:

1. Take three deep breaths. (inhale for 4 seconds, hold for 4 seconds, exhale for 4 seconds)

2. Walk around indoors or outdoors and use four of your senses to find:

- *4 things* I can see
- *3 things* I can touch
- *2 things* I can hear
- *1 thing* I can smell

3. Afterward, take a moment to reflect. It may help if you think about questions, such as:

- Was one sense easier to use than others?

    Yes _____   No _____

- Did I notice anything surprising?

    Yes _____   No _____

Here is what I noticed: _____

_____

_____

_____

_____

Change the System *(Page 72)*

EXERCISE: 5 Core Competencies of Social Emotional Learning

- Give a personal definition of each competency, i.e. *"What do I think this word means?"*

Self-Awareness	_____ _____ _____
Self-Management	_____ _____ _____
Social Awareness	_____ _____ _____
Responsible Decision Making	_____ _____ _____
Relationship Skills	_____ _____

Learn How to Learn *(Page 73)*

- Find the best ways for me to digest information and make it relatable to me
- Creatively break down information in ways that I will better understand what is being taught
- It is my duty to figure out some things on my own if and where I lack understanding

EXERCISE: Here are the best ways for me to understand or receive information:

_____

_____

_____

_____

Legacy

"Plan to leave something behind so your name will live on. No matter what, the game lives on." - NAS

Chapter 6 - The Hall of Fame

> - *"Set a bar for yourself... and then go over it!"*
> - Be courageous! I must recognize my power to take the necessary steps and be part of my own rescue; such as not waiting for anyone I aim to speak with to contact me first.

The Mental Hall of Fame: Individuals or groups who have inspired me and provided the necessary spark or guidance to improve my life.

EXERCISE: Below are the names of some of the individuals or groups who I would list in my Mental Hall of Fame.

- _____

- _____

- _____

College Completion Obstacles

List some factors or obstacles that can prevent college completion:

- _____

- _____

- _____

- _____

Post-High School Traps Students Should Aim To Avoid!

1. Unexpectedly having children without being properly prepared to take care of them
2. Getting caught up in illegal activity and spending years on probation, in prison, or killed
3. Choosing jobs or careers they hate or work at a company where they feel undervalued
4. Dropping out of college early and then experiencing one or more of the above

Chapter 7 - Be A Bridge

Work Harder? *(Page 85)*

- We all know that it is important to work hard, but that is not enough.
- *"Work smarter, not harder… but hard work will be necessary."*
- I can work hard and make little to no progress while wasting precious time and energy, or I can choose to work smart, be creative, and find efficient ways to arrive at my goal.

EXERCISE:

Ponder on this… Is there a better way to achieve the results I seek?

Like the story of the fly, am I banging against a window by attempting an impossible solution to my problem? Or, is there an open door that would help to resolve my issue(s) but I just have not realized it or taken advantage of the available opportunities or resources?

Here is one challenge I have been trying to address:

_____

Honestly, this is what I have done to resolve that challenge the same way, over and over again:

_____

_____

This is a person I know or learned about who has faced a similar challenge:

_____

One different approach that person, with a similar challenge, is doing or has done is:

_____

Alumni Mentorship *(Page 86)*

ASSIGNMENT: Find one, or multiple graduates from your school and get to know them. Alumni can provide you with great wisdom, even if they graduated decades ago.

Who did I find? _____

What will I do to get to know them? _____

When/where is our first conversation scheduled? _____

- **The Mentor... ME!** I am sure that I now have the power to give solid advice to students in younger grades than me. Maybe I can gain the opportunity to mentor at least one of them.
- **My story is important and deserves to be shared!** I should be honest about the mistakes I have made, but also include the multiple factors which have contributed to my success.

Community Service Events *(Page 90)*

QUESTION: What is something in my community that I am passionate about helping with?

_____

_____

CREATIVITY EXERCISE:
- Create a community service event. Use your imagination and write the idea! *(Who is being served? Who will help you? What are the required materials?)*

_____

_____

_____

_____

_____

EXERCISE: Fill in the blanks with the word that completes the acronym.

F = _____

Intently lock in on whatever mission, goal, or task I have in front of me.

A = _____

No more looking for someone else to blame when I fail or fall short!

C = _____

Knowing myself and believing in my abilities are the biggest factors needed to achieve positive results.

K = _____

My confidence will be backed and strengthened by the skills and experience I acquire.

T = _____

The present or NOW *(No Opportunity Wasted)* will always be the most important time of my life.

S = _____

I must create my own definition and version of this word and strive towards it with every decision I make.

Each One, Teach One *(Page 91)*

Circle the motivational message that most resonates with you.

I Will Believe In Myself At All Times!

Good Grades Are Worth Thousands Of Dollars!

Greatness Is Within Me!

I chose this statement because...

_____

_____

EXERCISE:

Use the messages above as inspiration. Use the space below to create your own motivational message poster that would inspire **YOU!**

Financial Freedom Fridays *(Page 92)*

EXERCISE:

- Write the names of five (5) millionaires or billionaires I automatically think of:

    1. _____

    2. _____

    3. _____

    4. _____

    5. _____

- If I wrote any athletes or entertainers above, I now must write five (5) millionaires or billionaires who are **NOT** professional athletes or entertainers:

    1. _____

    2. _____

    3. _____

    4. _____

    5. _____

NOTE: *"I do not have to become a millionaire or billionaire to be 'successful' BUT I should study the habits and decisions of millionaires and billionaires to learn more about wealth, investing, and value creation."*

Chapter 8 - Financial Literacy

- Obtaining and spending money is an example of the Universal Law of Reciprocity.
- "It's not just how about much money I make, it's about how much money I keep."

Blowing Your Money Away *(Page 97)*

EXERCISE: Check √ the response that best describes you.

- Many people immediately spend money once they receive it, but it is spent on trivial items.

    Do I do that?   Often _____   Rarely _____   Sometimes _____

- Since everything costs money, it makes sense to have more knowledge about money, as well as have an abundance of it.

    Do I strive to do that?   Yes _____   No _____   Sometimes _____

- Just because I can afford something, does not mean I should buy it.

    Do I think wisely before purchasing?   Often _____   Rarely _____   Sometimes _____

QUESTION: How do I save money?

_____

_____

_____

Sources versus Streams *(Page 99)*

EXERCISE: *(Fill in the blanks)*

- For most people to achieve financial freedom and retire comfortably, they will need multiple **sources** and **streams** of income.

    The main sources of income are **earned, passive,** and **residual.**

- _____ requires me to do physical work in order to get paid.

- _____ requires capital investment and then my money will continuously grow as long as it is invested.

- _____ comes from creating a certain type of monetizable idea, product, platform, or service – and then I receive payments from doing the work one time.

The Social Media Effect *(Page 100)*

- Social media affects my mind and can create an unrealistic comparison of myself to others.
- Stay away from scams or get rich quick schemes!
- I should do my own thorough research before blindly or impatiently jumping into anything. What may work for a friend may not necessarily work for me.

Sex is Expensive *(Page 101)*

"A person who can control their emotions and their sexual energy is powerful beyond measure."
Examples of how some humans spend money to have sex:
1. People buying flashy and overly priced items to attract partners
2. People buying and wearing certain clothing or body configurations to attract partners

Going Out? *(Page 102)*

Yes, it is good to have fun and enjoy life, but there is no need for mindless spending to celebrate everyday or every weekend. Those dollars add up quickly!

EXERCISE: The Going Out Game

Read the scenario below and respond to questions **a)** and **b)**

Your friend Justin says, ***"Let's go out and party tonight!"***

Write: a) the kinds of things you'll most likely pay for *(Ex: Uber, parking, club entry fee, premium drinks, tips, late night food, etc.)*
b) approximately how much each expense will cost.

a)_____ b) $_____   a)_____ b) $_____

a)_____ b) $_____   a)_____ b) $_____

a)_____ b) $_____   a)_____ b) $_____

Approximate Total $_____

QUESTION: How can I minimize or eliminate the costs of each item I listed above?

■ _____

■ _____

■ _____

Free? *(Page 103)*

- Living away from parents and on your own is a great freedom. But, always needing to spend most of your time & energy at work, just to pay bills... is not so "free"

- Do not feel rushed to move out of your parents' house immediately after graduation

- If manageable, staying with parents can allow me more time to save more money.
- This is a good strategy for a year or two, or as long as my family will allow.

EXERCISE: Based on the city you want to live in, write the average dollar amount of the given monthly adult expenses (Ex: average rent in Atlanta, GA for a 1 bdr apt. is $1,605 in 2025). An additional option is doing this exercise with a family member or mentor.

- Rent or Mortgage $_____
- Renters or Homeowners' insurance $_____
- Food (groceries and restaurants) $_____
- Cable, WiFi, and Phone Bill $_____
- Water Bill $_____
- Gas & Electric (Energy) Bill $_____
- Car payment, insurance, and maintenance $_____
- Parking, Uber, Gasoline $_____
- Subscriptions (e.g. Netflix or Hulu) $_____
- Gym or Club Memberships $_____
- Clothes $_____
- Flights & Vacations $_____
- Savings & Investing $_____
- Health & Life Insurance $_____
- Entertainment (recreation, theaters, athletic events, etc.) $_____
- Mental health and self-improvement $_____

Example Monthly Total $_____

QUESTION: Does this exercise give you an idea of how much money you may need to earn each month in your *'adulting'* life? What types of sustainable careers could provide that income?

_____

_____

Investing *(Page 106)*

- Put a certain percentage of money saved towards investing so your money can grow.
- Financially savvy people invest in a diverse portfolio of business ventures like small businesses, public companies listed on the stock market, real estate, and more.

Stocks *(Page 107)*

- Keep It Simple. Buy stock in companies that I already use daily or eventually want to use.
- The stock market goes through ups and downs, but it always goes back up. Be patient.
- **ETFs** – Exchange Traded Funds
- **Asset** – puts money in my pocket *(any useful thing or something that holds value)*
- **Liability** – takes money out of your pocket *(or costs you money)*

QUESTION: What do I need to learn more about investing and stocks? _____

_____

_____

_____

Credit and Debt *(Page 109)*

- America runs on credit. We use credit to get approved for apartments, purchase houses and cars, get jobs in certain industries, as well as get approved for personal & business loans. When I get a credit card – I SHOULD ONLY SPEND WHAT I CAN AFFORD!

- Try not to spend more than 30% of the card limit and pay the full payments on time!

- I can keep a clean credit report by paying my bills and loan payments on time. I will avoid interest charges by paying the full monthly balance before the due date.

QUESTION: What habits do I need to implement to manage my credit & debt?

_____

_____

_____

_____

Average? *(Page 111)*

- Do not be misled by the term 'average'. Being termed average depends on the category or the situation.

QUESTION: What is a category where I would classify as 'average' - and it's okay?

_____

College

"To think that in such a place, I led such a life."
– MIAMI UNIVERSITY ADOPTED QUOTE

Chapter 9 - The Transition to College

Is College Worth It? *(Page 116)*

- You may be surprised by how much you learn about different cultures, opportunities, companies, internships, or available roles after arriving on a college campus

EXERCISE: When considering college degree -vs- no degree, college can expand my:

- ■ _____

- ■ _____

- ■ _____

- ■ _____

Helpful Considerations When Determining My College Destination

- Compare my college choices – learn what certain schools offer that others do not.
- It is my responsibility to list the pros and cons of each college I am considering

- Tuition plus Room & Board Costs
- School Reputation or Notoriety
- Majors and Scholarships Offered
- Notable or Famous Alumni
- Campus Demographics

- Graduate Job Placement
- Updated Facilities & Safety Prioritization
- Student Organizations
- Study Abroad Opportunities
- Travel Expenses (visit home during breaks)

Where Do I Start? *(Page 117)*

- Choosing what type of institution I want to attend is another financial decision
  - i.e. 4-year university, community college, branch campus, etc. Some students start small and then transfer to a larger college that fits them.
- Deciding to attend a community college or branch campus option will save money, but I would miss the full experience that larger universities offer.

Financial Aid *(Page 118)*

- Apply for every scholarship under the sun! Go get that money to pay for school!
- Ask local organizations like fraternities and sororities, parents' jobs, churches, teachers, counselors, and mentors where to apply for certain scholarships
- FAFSA *(Free Application for Federal Student Aid)* helps schools determine what types of financial aid and how much financial aid students are able to receive based on personal and parental demographics & finances.

QUESTION: Who can help me properly fill out my FAFSA?

_____

_____

Employment *(Page 119)*

QUESTION: What type of jobs (on campus or near campus) can help me pay for my expenses and other wants while in college?

■_____   ■_____

■_____   ■_____

- After my freshman year, I can become a resident assistant and get free housing! This is an amazing opportunity to leverage and receive payment.

Health *(Page 119)*

- On campus there are a plethora of food options AND exercise options
- Walking or biking instead of taking the bus or using electric scooters can help keep me physically active

QUESTION: What are the main causes of the famous "Freshmen 15" pounds?

1. _____

2. _____

3. _____

Finding Mentors *(Page 119)*

- Mentors can help me reach my definition of success sooner.

   EXERCISE: Examples of people I can search out as mentors are:

   _____

   _____

   _____

   _____

Community *(Page 120)*

- Groups and organizations will allow me to build my community of friends who align with my passions and interests.

   EXERCISE: List the types of activities there are to engage in on college campuses

   _____

   _____

   _____

   _____

Textbooks *(Page 120)*

- *"Buy textbooks after two weeks of the new semester if you really need them"*
- This is a strategy that can work for some courses, but probably not each one

HELPFUL STEPS TO FOLLOW

   1. Go through the course syllabus and highlight key dates (exams, projects, etc.)
   2. Find and become friends with classmates who already have the textbook
   3. If I have to purchase the book for myself, I may find the needed book on campus or local libraries. *(wise to check them out ASAP due to limited quantities)*
   4. Renting textbooks can also save money if the option is available

Major Decision

- Many students change their major at least once during their college career.
- As early as possible, find others who have graduated with my major and ask how they leveraged their degrees.

QUESTION: What are some major industries that will always be needed in society?

_____

_____

_____

_____

_____

_____

Your Time and Self-Discipline *(Page 122)*

- Create a schedule and implement daily habits to instill self-discipline

EXERCISE: What are some examples of simple, good daily habits to adopt?

_____

_____

_____

_____

QUESTION: What are some of the most valuable tools I can have in college?

_____

_____

_____

I Must Find Time for Myself

- Spending time alone has great benefits such as time to be more productive, adapt to my new environment, and explore personal interests.

It Would Be Wise to Find a Hobby

- Only studying 24/7 can lead to burnout. A hobby is anything I think is fun and can free my mind when I'm not in class.

Coursework *(Page 123)*

- A helpful option is using voice recording while I take handwritten notes in class.

  Why? _____

  _____

- I should take advantage of office hours with my professors and teacher's assistants.

  Why? _____

  _____

- I should speak with my advisors frequently to ensure I am on the proper track to graduate.

  Why? _____

  _____

- Find credit transfer opportunities! **Why?**

  _____

  _____

- When studying for exams, find peers who understand the material.

  Why? _____

  _____

- Finals week! I should prepare for final exams well before the end of each semester.

  Why? _____

  _____

- Keep my self-talk positive *(write examples)*

  - _____

  - _____

  - _____

Chapter 10 - My Freshmen and Sophomore Years

Adjustment Phase *(Page 127)*

- *"I will prioritize my studies and my future! Expectations of attending parties, binge drinking, and other temptations may be faced. However, I still have classes, exams, a solid GPA to establish, rest to get, and responsibilities to manage. Because of this, there are some things and some people I will have to tell no."*

Freshman Year: Academics *(Page 130)*

- Attending a predominantly white institution forced the author to develop the ability to adapt and succeed in any environment, regardless of racial demographics, after graduating from a predominantly Black high school.

Some Benefits of Attending College:

1. Exposure to_____

2. Exposure to_____

3. Exposure to_____

EXERCISE: True -or- False

Mark with an **X** the appropriate answer to each statement below.

- Studying in college is different than in high school
    True ____ False ____

- Most college courses are three credit hours. Some may be higher.
    True ____ False ____

- Pulling *'all-nighters' (staying up all night to study or complete a project)* is mandatory.
    True ____ False ____

- Depending upon my major, there can be many internship opportunities available.
    True ____ False ____

- I can only apply for scholarships when entering my freshmen year.
    True ____ False ____

Résumé Tips *(Page 134)*

Résumé Definition: A snapshot of my professional self that I use to showcase my experiences with the aim of scheduling interviews and obtaining job offers.

EXERCISE:

(Fill in the blanks) A resume should include the following:

1. My _____ in large print.

2. My mailing address, _____ and _____

3. Bold _____ and minimal _____

4. My previous and current _____, including my major and _____

5. My _____ and volunteer _____

6. A summary of my _____ or _____

7. My work experience, using _____ and well-crafted

_____

CREATE MY RÉSUMÉ ACTIVITY: *(write answers & thoughts on lines)*

When is my expected graduation year?

What have I achieved in life so far? (Honor roll? Top in class ranking? Champion? Perfect Attendance? Executive title or position in an organization? A "high" GPA?)

What experiences do I have? (Previous or current jobs? "Cool" opportunities? Sports? Skills? Volunteering? Leadership?)

_____

_____

_____

_____

_____

_____

Taking a Break? *(Page 135)*

- **CONSIDER THIS:** Most students who take a break from college, never return. Although college is not "easy", graduating is worth the struggle! Most who choose to drop out are not working in their preferred career field or earning their desired salary.

Freshman Year: Spring Semester *(Page 135)*

- I am a valuable asset... **"I AM THE PRIZE!"**
  Below are the benefits **I** can bring to a college. *(ex: high GPA, creative ideas, athlete, etc.)*

- ▪ _____

- ▪ _____

- ▪ _____

Sophomore Year: Academics *(Page 138)*

- Establish a routine that makes school, work, and other responsibilities easier to juggle.
- Stay focused on the big picture you have envisioned your future to be.

  EXERCISE:

  Unscramble the Definition: 'Delayed Gratification'

  later. - immediate - will - come - reward - that - The - ability
  greater - for - a - postpone - exchange - to - pleasure - in

  _____

  _____

  _____

Sophomore Year: Athletics *(Page 127)*

- Proper nutrition, adequate sleep, and choosing to not consume harmful substances are key components for optimal health and performance
- Make smart decisions that do not put your scholarships at risk!
- You might cry tears of joy after achieving some of your goals!

- Remember you are a human with emotions who plays a sport/participates in activities for various reasons (typically for internal happiness at the start). Yes, achieving in them can lead to great external and financial benefits, but always remember to take care of your mental health and know you can redefine yourself at any moment by utilizing the skills you learn within and outside of sports or your activities of choice. (music, theatre, cooking, etc.)

Chapter 11 - My Junior Year

- It does not always matter what other people think. Governing my life by what others think can sometimes hold me back from realizing my vision.

My First Apartment *(Page 144)*

- Choosing the right roommate(s) is critical to my peace. *"Just because people are my friends does not mean I should live with them."*

QUESTION: What are traits I should learn about the person(s) I am considering rooming with before I agree to accept them? *(i.e. personal character, cleanliness, dependability, honesty, consideration of others, etc.)*

_____

_____

_____

Trauma, Fear and Emotions *(Page 145)*

- I must work on myself first! I am my greatest asset; especially my mental health!
- Therapy no longer has a negative stigma associated with it. Not addressing stress and other emotional challenges can lead to unhealthy coping mechanisms.

QUESTIONS:

- How can I benefit from taking time to honestly self-reflect on decisions I have made and how they have impacted my life?

_____

_____

_____

- What is the greatest lesson I have learned through personal reflection?

_____

_____

_____

EXERCISE: Unscramble each answer below

-   Some of the things people are afraid of are...

-   celeniS _____

-   rHia sosl _____

-   mntearsabErms _____

-   builPc kskeiangp _____

-   ineBg neloA _____

-   theaD _____

The Value of Internships *(Page 149)*

EXERCISE:

What does an internship provide? *(Fill in the blanks)*

√ An opportunity _____

_____

√ Real on-the-job training _____

_____

√ Networking with experienced _____

_____

√ An opportunity to increase _____

_____

_____

√ A chance to build _____

_____

√ An opportunity to figure out _____

_____

Prepare for the Job Fair QUESTION: *(Page 153)*

What things can I do to help make myself **stand out** to perspective employers at a job fair?

_____

_____

_____

EXERCISE:

Highly Effective Interview Questions – for ME to ask the interviewer *(Page 154)*

1. _____

2. _____

3. _____

4. _____

5. _____

6. _____

7. _____

8. _____

9. _____

Graduate School Acceptance *(Page 158)*

- Having good grades and having an advocate who can speak positively on my behalf are examples of factors that can lead to my acceptance into a graduate program I desire.

- If it takes a college student more than 4 years to graduate... it is OKAY! The degree only signifies completion, not how long it took to complete it.

- Depending on the school, a student may need to take an average of 16 credit hours per semester in order to graduate in 4 years. Summer courses might be necessary.

My Internship Experiences *(Page 159)*

- An internship experience can help me gain a better perspective of what I really want for my future.

- Sometimes the internship experience is more about getting to know the culture and the people within a company. i.e. networking and relationship building

- If I come from a challenging or unhealthy home environment/neighborhood, I should aim to become the change I want to see for my life.

Additional Advice

- FIND OPPORTUNITIES TO STUDY ABROAD AND WAYS TO GET IT PAID FOR!!! Most students go to college in their hometown or home state and rarely get to experience life outside of their home country. GET OUT IF YOU CAN! Whether you choose a college outside of your home state or not, try to obtain an internship in a different city or state than where your college or hometown is located. This will offer you a completely new experience and network.

- Studying abroad can occur during the summer time or during a full semester in the Fall or Spring.

Chapter 12 - My Senior Year

- It is beneficial to read books outside of class to help develop your mindset and skillset.
- Be strategic while leveraging your strengths and relationships to produce positive results.

Experiences with Cultural Bias *(Page 166)*

QUESTION:

- *"You would be the perfect thief!"* What makes this a harmfully biased statement made by people of other ethnicities about a role that could be played by a Black American man?

_____

_____

_____

Greek? *(Page 166)*

QUESTIONS:

- The number one rule when joining a Greek-lettered social organization is

  _____.

- There can be some cons to joining Fraternities or Sororities. Time constraints and new

  responsibilities can cause relationships to _____.

The Benefits of Joining Greek Organizations *(Page 168)*

- Some benefits are:

  - Gaining lifelong brothers or sisters; locally, nationally, and globally who provide a sense of belonging thanks to commonalities

  - Fraternity brothers or sorority sisters can be my resources for information and help open doors for jobs and/or favors needed.

  - Always being able to connect with and learn from members who are older than me, as well as, those who are younger than me

Words of Wisdom *(Page 170)*

QUESTION: What did Frederick Douglass say about 'Struggle'?

_____

_____

What stood out most to me after reading this section?

_____

_____

_____

Meeting a Legend *(Page 173)*

- Advice from a highly successful business owner, Dr. J.C. Baker: *"... it is important to get things done instead of just talking about them"*

EXERCISE: What is something I need to get DONE that I have only talked about doing?

_____

_____

_____

Bet on Yourself *(Page 174)*

QUESTIONS: Was there a time I missed an opportunity to bet on myself?

_____ Yes   _____ No   **(Check √ your response)**

What lesson did I learn from this section? _____

_____

_____

How can I apply this lesson to myself? _____

_____

_____

Chapter 13 - My Fifth and Final Year

Questions We Must Ask Ourselves *(Page 178)*

- Do I _____?

- Do I _____?

- How great do I _____?

Did these questions spark you to ask any further questions? If yes, write them.

_____

_____

_____

Mr. Figure It Out *(Page 179)*

- There will be times when I have to be creative and willing to find whatever is necessary to get what is needed to arrive at my destination.

My Last Collegiate Track Seasons *(Page 180)*

> *"I am confident in my abilities to achieve my big goals! I will speak my vision into existence as though it has already happened! I will not blindly imitate what I see from public icons. I desire to learn better ways of professionally presenting myself!"*

QUESTION: What does this quote mean to you? *"Turn my fear into fuel"*

_____

_____

Graduation Time! *(Page 183)*

- Vocally participating in classes is part of my final grade
- Purposefully sitting in the front of the classroom can be a great strategy. **Why?**

_____

_____

- I should think carefully about how I can leverage the degree I achieve **(transferable skills)**
- Choosing to become an employee can be a good part of my plan on the journey to achieve my life dreams

QUESTION: What does the statement below mean to me?

- *"I will do what I have to do, until I can do what I truly want to do."*

_____

_____

_____

QUESTION: *(Page 186)*

- What is sometimes necessary for those who desire to become a full-time entrepreneur?

■ _____

Advice about Transferable Skills

- The author achieved two degrees in Accounting but chose Education as his career path
- The author uses the skills he learned from studying Accounting by:
  - Being skeptical like an Accountant means to 'Question Everything' and always dive deeper in search of the truth or the connection & practical use of information
  - Accountants understand the use and importance of compartmentalization. Simply meaning, there is a time and place for everything. Money within companies and households has various purposes and belongs in different buckets for various uses. This applies to real life via proper time management for task completion, emotional expression, friend groups, and more
  - Paying attention to details is critical! One wrongly placed number on an income statement, balance sheet, or cash flow statement, can change the whole perception and trajectory of a business. This relates to personal & professional life by how we must be mindful of how we present ourselves and what we choose to attach ourselves with

Think about and write some of the transferable skills from your future major:

_____

_____

_____

Post-College Whirlwind

"Absorb what is useful. Discard what is not.
Add what is uniquely your own." - Bruce Lee

Chapter 14 - Graduated from College...Now What?

- **Most college graduates choose the employee route and begin working their career**

    1. Their first job after college is typically in an industry that aligns with their degree
    2. Some students interview with multiple companies before and after graduation
    3. Their next step is often obtaining solo housing

- **It is wise to focus on more than just salary when choosing an employer**

    1. Work environment & benefits like health insurance and vacation days are important
    2. You probably will not stay with your first employer forever. Keep your options open.
    3. Some graduates choose to stay in school and achieve a higher degree
    4. Some graduates start businesses and leverage the resources they gained in college

The Business Hospital *(Page 192)*

- Most problems that small businesses face consist of weak internal controls, poor salesmanship, and the inability to clearly articulate their value propositions.

EXERCISE: *(Fill in the blanks)*

Lessons learned from *'Foot to Pavement'* style of sales *(Page 193)*

- It is a _____ game

- I must have _____ to say what _____ said

- I must clearly articulate my _____ of receiving the sale

- There are _____ to ask to get anyone to engage in _____

- Learn to simultaneously listen to _____ AND what they _____

- Learn how to overcome objections and _____

QUESTION: What are some key lessons that Dr. Baker taught? *(Pages 192 - 195)*

_____

_____

_____

QUESTION: In businesses without many employees, what is the owner responsible for?

_____

_____

_____

My Journey to the 2020 Olympics *(Page 199)*

- "Unhealthy comparison is the thief of joy." **Agree or Disagree? Explain further.**

_____

_____

_____

Fraternity Benefits and Social Media *(Page 200)*

- If I hold on to fearful thoughts, I am blocking my blessings! BE COURAGEOUS!

    QUESTION: What lessons can I learn from reading this section? *(Page 200)*

_____

_____

_____

Injuries, Competing, and Traveling *(Page 200)*

- Injuries are the somewhat sad part of sports. However, there are many lessons to be learned from injuries, especially during the time an athlete is forced to reflect & recover.
- Competition is fun! But it can also cause some people to overstress or go against their morals. Remain true to yourself and remember that you are your biggest competitor.
- Travel internationally at least once to see and experience what truly occurs outside of your home country instead of solely relying on what others say.

My Experience in Politics *(Page 204)*

QUESTION: What process and activities did the author go through while campaigning for a position on the school board?

_____

_____

_____

A Global Pandemic *(Page 206)*

- Technological advancements resulting from the pandemic have enabled some businesses to serve their clients and customers from anywhere with internet access.

EXERCISE: List some changes that occurred in my life or within my immediate family during the COVID pandemic.

_____

_____

_____

_____

- During the pandemic, some people took the opportunity to reevaluate their lives and create different career paths.

- An example of someone I know *(or heard about)* who made a change in their career or business as a result of the pandemic is:

_____

_____

_____

_____

_____

Chapter 15 - Kenny's Lifestyle Changes

Still Running Track? *(Page 210)*

- Everything has a time and place, and no one should place a limit on their self-belief.

The Realities of Entrepreneurship Passion Statement: The author wrote a note to himself proclaiming his passion: *"I am a creative problem solver who understands the importance of finances."*

QUESTION: What is the quote made by Buku Ibraheem? *(Page 214)*

_____

EXERCISE: Circle the best answer to the statement below.

- Another aspect of entrepreneurship is the high rate of failure due to:

   a) Lack of funds

   b) Ineffective business models

   c) Inability to sell or inadequate teams

   d) All of the above

Educational Passion *(Page 214)*

EXERCISE: Write how you think these ideas might help your school or school district

1. Increase the number of opportunities and resources available to students before & after graduation and help students open their minds to take advantage of them.

_____

_____

_____

2. Gain strategic partnerships with mentor groups and local businesses to improve financial literacy that is applicable for students.

_____

_____

_____

3. Partner with HBCUs and organizations that focus on solutions to increase the number of and retention of Black American teachers.

_____

_____

_____

Nutritional Change *(Page 217)*

- Do my own research and gather information from multiple, reputable sources.
- Apply what I find by trying and eliminating certain foods to find what is best for me.
- Be conscious about what I put in my body because I only get one.

SOMETHING TO THINK ABOUT:

Neighborhoods that do not have businesses or restaurants that promote health, wealth, or wellness are places called *"the trap"* **(Page 218)**

Why? _____

_____

QUESTION: What are processed foods?

_____

_____

_____

Monk Mode *(Page 220)*

ASSIGNMENT:

The author shaved his head bald as a symbol of change and for a fresh start. Talk with two (2) adults over the age of 30. Ask these adults *"Did you do anything in your life to symbolize a 'change' or a 'fresh start' which some people may have considered drastic?"*
Write what you learned from your discussions.

_____

_____

_____

_____

TIPS TO AID IN MY SUCCESS:

1. Listening - How can I improve?

_____

_____

_____

2. Patience - How can I improve?

_____

_____

_____

3. Self-control - How can I improve?

_____

_____

_____

4. Discipline - How can I improve?

_____

_____

_____

5. Continuous growth in knowledge, wisdom, and understanding - How can I improve?

_____

_____

_____

_____

EVERYDAY HABITS FOR SUCCESS

PERSONAL ASSIGNMENT:

- Beginning today, choose at least two (2) habits listed below and implement them. Then, choose and implement two (2) other habits each day until all ten (10) habits have been implemented.

1. Consistently getting 0.0001% better at something
2. Getting off my phone before bed
3. Rising out of bed earlier than most
4. Meditation
5. Metacognition

6. Staying hydrated with seeded fruits & water
7. Writing in my gratitude journal
8. Writing down my goals
9. Visualization
10. Deep breathing

Day #1 HABITS

- _____
- _____

Day #2 HABITS

- _____
- _____

Day #3 HABITS

- _____
- _____

Day #4 HABITS

- _____
- _____

Day #5 HABITS

- _____
- _____

At the conclusion of the five days, reflect and write about what you experienced:

_____

_____

_____

_____

_____

_____

QUICK ADVICE

EXERCISE: From the list of advice given, list six (6) points that most resonate with you.

1. _____

2. _____

3. _____

4. _____

5. _____

6. _____

Dear My Younger Self:

_____

_____

_____

_____

_____

_____

_____

_____

_____

_____

_____

_____

_____

_____

_____

_____

Dear My Younger Self:

_____

_____

_____

_____

_____

_____

_____

_____

_____

_____

_____

_____

_____

_____

_____

_____

Dear My Younger Self:

_____

_____

_____

_____

_____

_____

_____

_____

_____

_____

_____

_____

_____

_____

_____

_____

_____

Dear My Younger Self:

_____

_____

_____

_____

_____

_____

_____

_____

_____

_____

_____

_____

_____

_____

_____

_____

_____

_____

Dear My Younger Self:

_____

_____

_____

_____

_____

_____

_____

_____

_____

_____

_____

_____

_____

_____

_____

_____

_____

_____

_____

Dear My Younger Self:

_____

_____

_____

_____

_____

_____

_____

_____

_____

_____

_____

_____

_____

_____

_____

_____

Dear My Younger Self:

Dear My Younger Self:

_____

_____

_____

_____

_____

_____

_____

_____

_____

_____

_____

_____

_____

_____

_____

_____

_____

Dear My Younger Self:

_____

_____

_____

_____

_____

_____

_____

_____

_____

_____

_____

_____

_____

_____

_____

_____

_____

_____